All About
NOTHING

Elizabeth Rusch & Elizabeth Goss

Charlesbridge

What do you know
about nothing?

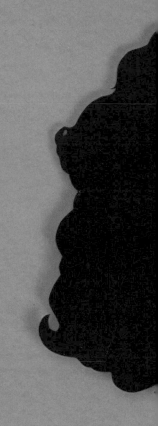

Nothing is the space around
and between everything—
your hand, a pet, or even a city.

It's hard to read
without nothing.

NOTHING
HELPSYOU
SEEWHERE
WORDS
BEGIN
ANDEND

Nothing grabs your attention!

And changes
the way you look.

Outer space is mostly
nothing.

That's why we call
it space.

Even when you can't see nothing,
you can feel it.

Nothing can be that moment
before something exciting happens.

in a busy day.

Nothing even makes music.

For what is a song
without some silence?

You can have too little of nothing.

Or just the right amount.

The most amazing things
can happen
when there is nothing.

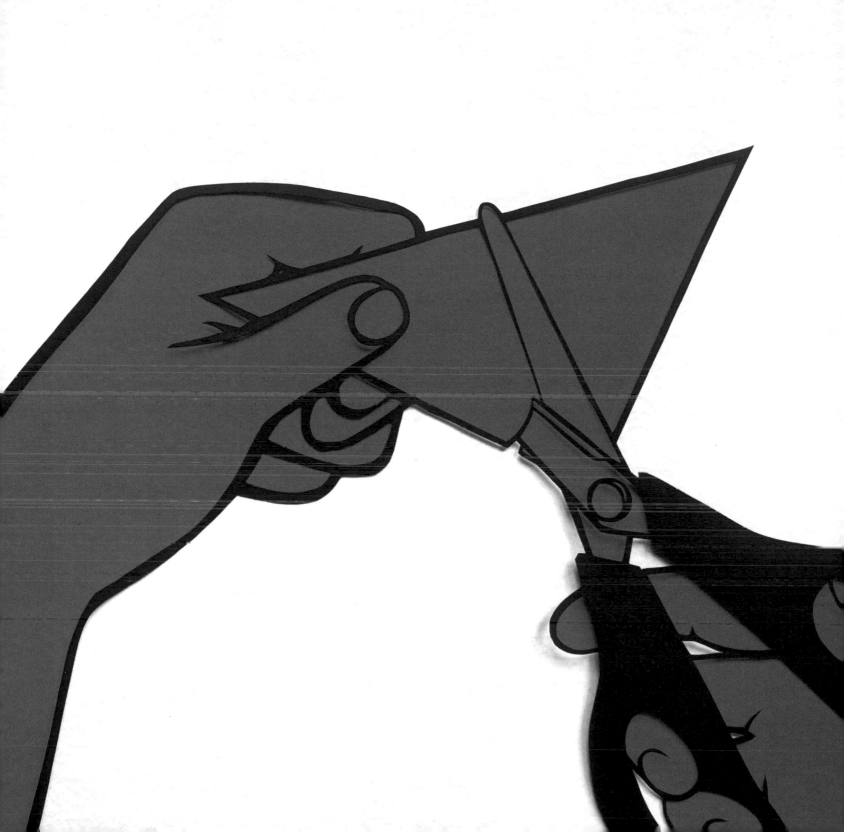

Because nothing

is really something!

ABOUT NEGATIVE SPACE

Nothingness can be where creativity blooms, especially in art. Look around. Maybe you see a table, a chair, or a bike. Now, instead of looking at those objects, notice the space inside, next to, and around them. This nothingness is called negative space.

It's easy to see negative space when you carve a jack-o'-lantern. The positive space is the pumpkin. When you cut pieces away, you create negative space.

You can do this with paper and scissors, too. Fold a sheet of paper in half. Cut a half circle and a half banana from the folded side and another half circle from the edge above. When you unfold the paper, you'll see a smiling face. In fact, all the art in this book was created by cutting paper to highlight positive and negative space!

Artists and designers pay a lot of attention to negative space. When drawing a rabbit, an artist considers: Should the rabbit be big and in the middle of the page, taking up a lot of space? Or should it be small or off to one side? How does the empty space around the little rabbit make you feel?

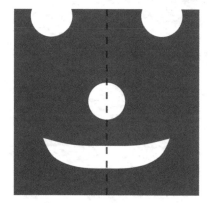

Negative space can create a game of hide-and-seek. A classic example is Rubin's Vase. In the picture to the right, do you see an elegant vase? Look again. If you focus on the space around the vase, you might see something different!

Nothingness can help you draw a donut without drawing the donut. Color in the hole first. Then color in all the space around the donut.

Look closely at the branch of a tree. Now notice the spaces around the branch and its leaves. What shapes do they make?

Try sketching the space around objects. You might be surprised at how interesting your drawings are. That's because we're not used to noticing negative space. When we focus on nothing, we see the world in a whole new way.

MORE ABOUT NOTHING

There is more nothing in your life than you might realize. Nothing is a long expanse of sky over a prairie, an empty bowl after all the ice cream has been eaten, even the spaces between plants in a garden.

Music depends on nothingness. Imagine a song where all the notes and lyrics run together without a pause or rest. The silence between notes can be as powerful as the notes themselves. Moments of silence, of nothing, can mean everything.

Nothingness in your day gives you time to relax, breathe, and dream. Imagine a day so busy with activities that your head spins. Now imagine a free afternoon, a quiet room, an empty park. Try adding some nothingness to your day by pausing for a moment, closing your eyes, and just breathing.

To the artist in all of us—L. R.

For Florence, with love—L. G.

At the time of publication, all URLs printed in this book were accurate and active. Charlesbridge, the author, and the illustrator are not responsible for the content or accessibility of any website.

Published by Charlesbridge
9 Galen Street
Watertown, MA 02472
(617) 926-0329
www.charlesbridge.com

Printed in China
(hc) 10 9 8 7 6 5 4 3 2 1

Illustrations done in cut paper
Display and text type set in Quicksand by
    Andrew Paglinawan
Printed by 1010 Printing International Limited in
    Huizhou, Guangdong, China
Production supervision by Jennifer Most Delaney
Designed by Jon Simeon

Library of Congress Cataloging-in-Publication Data
Names: Rusch, Elizabeth, author. | Goss, Elizabeth, illustrator.
Title: All about nothing / Elizabeth Rusch; illustrated by Elizabeth Goss.
Description: Watertown, MA: Charlesbridge, 2023. | Audience: Ages 4–8 | Audience: Grades K–1 | Summary: "This concept book introduces young children to the role of nothingness and negative space in their world."—Provided by publisher.
Identifiers: LCCN 2022003128 (print) | LCCN 2022003129 (ebook) | ISBN 9781623543525 (hardcover) | ISBN 9781632893222 (ebook)
Subjects: LCSH: Nothing (Philosophy)—Juvenile literature.
Classification: LCC BD398 .R87 2023 (print) | LCC BD398 (ebook) | DDC 111/.5—dc23/eng/20220725
LC record available at https://lccn.loc.gov/2022003128
LC ebook record available at https://lccn.loc.gov/2022003129

Special thanks to editor Alyssa Mito Pusey and designer Jon Simeon for the fun and productive collaboration—The Lizzes